Test Booklet

Starter

Third Edition

Person to Person

Communicative Speaking and Listening Skills

D1344535

CHe

Jack C. Richards

Andy London

CD INSIDE BACK COVER

OXFORD
UNIVERSITY PRESS

198 Madison Avenue
New York, NY 10016 USA

Great Clarendon Street, Oxford OX2 6DP UK

Oxford University Press is a department of the University of Oxford.
It furthers the University's objective of excellence in research, scholarship,
and education by publishing worldwide in

Oxford New York

Auckland Cape Town Dar es Salaam Hong Kong Karachi
Kuala Lumpur Madrid Melbourne Mexico City Nairobi
New Delhi Shanghai Taipei Toronto

With offices in

Argentina Austria Brazil Chile Czech Republic France Greece
Guatemala Hungary Italy Japan Poland Portugal Singapore
South Korea Switzerland Thailand Turkey Ukraine Vietnam

OXFORD and OXFORD ENGLISH are registered trademarks of
Oxford University Press

Executive Publisher: Nancy Leonhardt
Senior Acquisitions Editor: Chris Balderston
Senior Editor: Patricia O'Neill
Assistant Editor: Kate Schubert
Art Director: Maj-Britt Hagsted
Layout Artist: Julie Macus
Production Manager: Shanta Persaud
Production Controller: Eve Wong

ISBN-13: 978 0 19 430225 8 (Starter Test Booklet)
ISBN-10: 0 19 430225 3 (Starter Test Booklet)
ISBN-13: 978 0 19 430224 1 (Starter Test Booklet with CD)
ISBN-10: 0 19 430224 5 (Starter Test Booklet with CD)

Printed in Hong Kong.

10 9 8 7 6 5 4 3 2

CONTENTS

INTRODUCTION

Person to Person, 3rd edition, Starter Test Booklet is designed for unit-by-unit evaluation of students' mastery of the Student Book. The tests may be given in a language laboratory or in a regular classroom with a CD player, and they are easily administered to large or small groups of students. Teachers may use the tests to assign grades or to identify areas in which students need additional assistance.

This test package includes photocopiable student test sheets, an answer key, and an audio script of the recorded portions of the tests. A CD on the inside back cover of the Test Booklet contains the recordings needed to administer the tests.

The test items are based on the listening and speaking activities presented in the Student Book. Listen to This assesses listening ability, while Give It A Try assesses speaking ability. Both sections are presented in multiple-choice, true-false, or matching formats.

The Tests

Each unit test is divided into two sections and is worth a total of 20 points. This format was chosen to make it easier for teachers of large classes to administer and score their students' tests.

The tests can be adapted according to the needs of the teacher and students. Teachers may wish to use only certain sections of a test because of time constraints. It may also be appropriate in some cases to play one part of a test twice, depending on the students' level and the intended use of the test results.

Timing

Each unit test is about 10–15 minutes long. Actual administration time, including set-up and collection of materials at the end of the test, may run ten minutes longer.

Giving the Test

Before the students arrive, teachers should photocopy test sheets for themselves and all of their students. When the class has started, teachers distribute the test sheets and have the students write their names and the date on them. Teachers then read aloud the instructions for the first section and play the CD. (They may wish to play each recording twice.) Before playing the second section, teachers should go over the instructions and make sure students understand them. Once the listening section is completed, teachers can then have students complete the speaking section. This section presents the language and functions practiced in the Student Book, and students select the answer that best completes the sample conversation. When the test is finished, teachers collect the test sheets from the class. They should check to make sure they receive one test sheet from each student and that each test sheet has the correct name written on it.

Scoring

Space is provided at the end of each section to write the students' scores for that section. In addition, space is provided at the top of the test sheet to write the students' total score. A scale of 20 points is used to make it easy to convert the scores to grades.

Teachers may wish to go over the test in class so that students can see their errors and review any difficult areas. The test results can help teachers determine where additional practice is needed. When assigning grades, it is most beneficial to use the test results in conjunction with other types of assessment, such as the speaking activities in the Let's Talk sections of the Student Book. A wide variety of assessments will give teachers a fuller picture of their students' skills and strengths.

Name: _____ Date: _____

LISTEN TO THIS

Track 2 **1.** People are talking. Listen and write the letter of the correct answer.

1. Won-gyu ____
2. Ted ____
3. Lisa ____
4. Emily ____
5. Dan ____

a. Wu
b. Miller
c. Kozo
d. Moon
e. Robinson

5

Track 3 **2.** People are talking. Are these statements true or false? Listen and check (✓) the correct answer.

	True	False
1. Nat wants to know who Noriko is.	☐	☐
2. Noriko and Mari are sisters.	☐	☐
3. Nat thinks Mari is pretty.	☐	☐
4. Nat doesn't want to meet Mari.	☐	☐
5. Mari and Nat are in the same math class.	☐	☐

5

1. People are talking. Number the sentences in the correct order.

1. ___   A: Oh! It's time for class! See you!
2. ___   B: Pretty good. How was your weekend?
3. ___   A: Hi, Judy. How are things going?
4. ___   B: Relaxing. I stayed home and watched TV.
5. ___   A: Great, thanks. How was yours?

`5`

2. Write the letter of the correct answer.

1. Is his name Mark? ___
2. Shinsuke, this is my friend Ben. ___
3. Who's she? ___
4. Is he from Taipei? ___
5. Is Sun-hee in your class? ___

a. No, he's from Beijing.
b. Her name is Keiko.
c. Yes, it is.
d. Yes, she is.
e. Nice to meet you.

`5`

Name: _____ Date: _____

LISTEN TO THIS

Track 4

1. People are talking about objects. Listen and write the letter of the correct answer.

1. It is warm. ___
2. They are from her mother. ___
3. It is heavy. ___
4. They are for her house. ___
5. They are for basketball. ___

a. sneakers
b. keys
c. a backpack
d. a jacket
e. earrings

[5]

Track 5

2. People are looking for objects. Listen and write the letter of the correct answer.

1. a green shirt ___
2. a cell phone ___
3. a bag ___
4. keys ___
5. sunglasses ___

a. next to the couch
b. in her jacket's pocket
c. on top of her head
d. on the kitchen table
e. in the closet

[5]

GIVE IT A TRY

1. People are talking. Number the sentences in the correct order.

1. ___ B: They're David's.
2. ___ B: No, they aren't.
3. ___ A: Oh, they're really nice.
4. ___ A: Are these your sunglasses?
5. ___ A: Whose are they?

[5]

2. Complete each sentence and circle the letter of the correct answer.

1. Have you _____ my green T-shirt?
   a. drank
   b. eaten
   c. seen

2. Your books are _____ the table.
   a. around
   b. on
   c. between

3. I need a new _____ of shoes.
   a. six
   b. green
   c. pair

4. Don't forget your _____ or you will be locked out.
   a. keys
   b. pencil
   c. sunglasses

5. I just _____ a new pair of earrings. Do you like them?
   a. met
   b. talked to
   c. bought

5

Name: _____   Date: _____

LISTEN TO THIS

Track 6   **1.** People are joining a sports club. Listen and write the letter of the correct answer.

1. Brian Davidson ___   a. weighs 58 kilos, likes baseball
2. Hyun-young Choi ___   b. 180 cm tall, likes basketball
3. Anna Nelson ___   c. doesn't like sports, is 20 years old
4. Shoji Fujimori ___   d. is 22 years old, weighs 60 kilos
5. Pavel Hoffman ___   e. is 21 years old, runs track

5

Track 7   **2.** People are talking. Are these statements true or false? Listen and check (✓) the correct answer.

	True	False
1. Andy has one older sister.	☐	☐
2. Li-wei loves baseball.	☐	☐
3. Andy likes reggae music.	☐	☐
4. Li-wei has four younger sisters.	☐	☐
5. Andy is 26 years old.	☐	☐

5

GIVE IT A TRY

1. Complete each conversation and circle the letter of the correct answer.

1. A: Tell me about your family.
   B: Well, I come from a _____ family.

   a. biggest-sized
   b. medium
   c. medium-sized

2. **A:** Do you have any brothers and sisters?

   B: Yes, I _____.

   a. am an only child
   b. have three of them
   c. have one sister and two brothers

3. **A:** How tall are you?

   B: I'm _____ tall.

   a. 16
   b. 165 centimeters
   c. 80 kilos

4. **A:** What do your parents do?

   B: _____.

   a. My parents are retired
   b. My dad's name is Shin and my mom's name is Aki
   c. My father is 48 and my mother is 50

5. **A:** What are you interested in?

   B: _____.

   a. Not really
   b. I like nature
   c. I don't like shopping

5

2. Write the letter of the correct answer.

1. What kind of movies do you like? ___
2. Do you like to travel? ___
3. What are your favorite hobbies? ___
4. Are you interested in sports? ___
5. What is your favorite type of music? ___

a. I like traveling, cooking, and baseball.
b. Well, my favorites are comedies.
c. I love classical.
d. Yes, I am.
e. Yes, I love it. In fact, I'm going to Nepal next week.

5

Name: _____ Date: _____

LISTEN TO THIS

Track 8   **1.** People are talking at a party. Listen and write the letter of the correct answer.

1. Mary ___
2. Mr. Davidson ___
3. Jessie ___
4. David Kline ___
5. So-hyun ___

a. long brown hair, red dress
b. short, long black hair, pink skirt
c. blonde, yellow T-shirt
d. curly black hair, green sweater
e. short, heavy, wearing glasses

5

Track 9   **2.** People are talking about gifts for family members. Listen and circle the letter of the correct answer.

1. Dad is getting a _____.
   a. red sunglasses
   b. blue coat
   c. striped tie
   d. gold watch

2. Jenny is getting a _____.
   a. cute silver earrings
   b. red dress
   c. scarf
   d. red coat

3. Jeremy is getting a _____.
   a. pair of shoes
   b. gray suit
   c. pair of sunglasses
   d. brown backpack

4. Allison is getting a _____.
   a. gold watch
   b. blue purse
   c. pair of jeans
   d. cell phone

5. Grandma is getting a _____.
   a. silver watch
   b. gold earrings
   c. black scarf
   d. silver bracelet

5

GIVE IT A TRY

1. Complete each sentence with the letter of the correct answer.

1. What did you ___ Sung-ho for Valentine's Day?   a. got
2. Well, it's hard to ___ for men on Valentine's Day.   b. get
3. So, I ___ him a gift certificate for a music store.   c. shop
4. Did he ___ it?   d. think
5. I ___ so, he seemed happy.   e. like

2. Complete each sentence and circle the letter of the correct answer.

1. Takao is tall and thin with _____ hair.
   a. dark black
   b. curling
   c. heavy

2. She is _____ a green sweater and blue jeans.
   a. like
   b. wearing
   c. think

3. Suzanne has long brown _____.
   a. hair
   b. eyes
   c. watch

4. It's so bright I can't see. Please hand me my _____.
   a. shirt
   b. sweater
   c. sunglasses

5. I need to study. Have you seen my _____?
   a. purse
   b. backpack
   c. watch

Name: _____   Date: _____

LISTEN TO THIS

Track 10　**1.** People are talking about their schedules. Listen and circle the letter of the correct answer.

1. What time did the speaker go to bed?
   a. 2:00 P.M.
   b. 10:30 P.M.
   c. 2:00 A.M.
   d. 12:00 A.M.

2. What time does the class end?
   a. 3:15
   b. 3:30
   c. 3:45
   d. 2:45

3. What time does the movie start?
   a. 8:00
   b. 7:45
   c. 8:15
   d. 8:30

4. What time does the speaker have to get up in the morning?
   a. 6:30 P.M.
   b. 6:45 A.M.
   c. 6:30 A.M.
   d. 7:00 P.M.

5. What time are the dinner reservations?
   a. 6:15
   b. 7:15
   c. 6:30
   d. 6:45

☐ 5

Track 11　**2.** People are talking after class. Are these statements true or false? Listen and check (✓) the correct answer.

	True	False
1. Jung-soon works on Sunday.	☐	☐
2. Minako can go to lunch with Toshi.	☐	☐
3. Eva went to Italy and got married.	☐	☐
4. Jade will go to a party on Saturday.	☐	☐
5. Hyun-gil is going to study all night.	☐	☐

☐ 5

GIVE IT A TRY

1. Complete each sentence with the letter of the correct answer.

1. What time do you usually ___ in the morning?   a. this weekend
2. I wake up around ___ every day.   b. Sunday
3. What are you going to do ___?   c. get up
4. I am going to ___ a movie on Saturday.   d. see
5. What are you doing on ___?   e. 6:00 A.M.

2. Complete each sentence and circle the letter of the correct answer.

1. I usually _____ TV on Sundays.
   a. make
   b. watch
   c. take

2. I _____ baseball. I try and see about 20 games a year.
   a. love
   b. see
   c. hate

3. I am _____ a party at my house this weekend.
   a. from
   b. having
   c. to

4. Would you _____ to go to lunch after class today?
   a. see
   b. be
   c. like

5. Do you _____ to go dancing this weekend?
   a. from
   b. want
   c. make

Name: _____ Date: _____

LISTEN TO THIS

Track 12

1. People are talking about what they do. Are these statements true or false? Listen and check (✓) the correct answer.

	True	False
1. Young-su is a teacher.	☐	☐
2. Julia is studying French.	☐	☐
3. Young-su is going to cooking school.	☐	☐
4. Julia likes her engineering class.	☐	☐
5. Julia is a really good cook.	☐	☐

5

Track 13

2. People are talking about their college professors. Listen and write the letter of the correct answer.

1. Professor Chen ___   a. interesting and funny
2. Professor Marx ___   b. easygoing and reliable
3. Professor Riddle ___   c. serious; unique teaching style
4. Professor Johnson ___   d. fascinating
5. Professor Houston ___   e. unreliable

5

GIVE IT A TRY

1. Complete each conversation and circle the letter of the correct answer.

1. **A:** What are you studying?
   B: I am studying _____ because I like designing my own clothes.

   a. business
   b. fashion
   c. biology

2. **A:** Do you like Mr. Brown?
   B: I love his class, he is a _____ teacher.

   a. wonderful
   b. so-so
   c. pretty bad

3. A: What's wrong, Val?
   B: I think I'm getting sick. I feel _____.

   a. awful
   b. OK
   c. pretty good

4. A: What are June and Greg like?
   B: They are so different. She is so shy and he is so _____.

   a. ingoing
   b. outgoing
   c. quiet

5. A: I really enjoy our _____ class.
   B: Me, too. I have always been fascinated with the past.

   a. math
   b. computer science
   c. history

   5

2. **Choose the correct response to each description. Write the letter of the correct answer.**

1. He's so friendly with everyone he meets. ___
2. She always makes me laugh. ___
3. I can always count on her. ___
4. It isn't easy for her to talk to other people. ___
5. He doesn't think anything is funny. ___

a. Yes, he's very serious.
b. Me, too. She's so funny.
c. I know. She's really shy.
d. I agree. She's reliable.
e. Yeah, he's really outgoing.

   5

Name: _____ Date: _____

LISTEN TO THIS

Track 14

1. People are talking about what they do on the weekend. Are these statements true or false? Listen and check (✓) the correct answer.

	True	False
1. Yoshi usually goes to see live music on Friday.	☐	☐
2. Sarah hasn't been to many Broadway shows.	☐	☐
3. Yoshi plays tennis on Saturday.	☐	☐
4. Yoshi often goes to Lincoln Center.	☐	☐
5. Sarah and Yoshi will go to the opera together.	☐	☐

5

Track 15

2. People are talking about their weekend. Listen and write the letter of the correct answer.

1. Tamara went to the City Museum and saw some ___.
2. On Saturday Tamara bought a new pair of ___.
3. Arun ___ a baseball game on Friday.
4. On Saturday Arun ___ his friends downtown.
5. Arun has a big ___ on Wednesday.

a. test
b. shoes
c. saw
d. met
e. exhibitions

5

GIVE IT A TRY

1. Complete each sentence and circle the letter of the correct answer.

1. I _____ like to go to a movie on the weekend.
   a. see
   b. feel
   c. usually

2. On Friday, I like to _____ my friends.
   a. know
   b. meet
   c. taste

3. My _____ thing to do is go to concerts on the weekend.
   a. favorite
   b. small
   c. large

4. I went _____ for a new jacket yesterday.
   a. buying
   b. living
   c. shopping

5. I _____ tickets to see a baseball game tomorrow.
   a. have
   b. having
   c. relaxed

`5`

2. **Complete each sentence with the letter of the correct answer.**

1. I am ___ to meet my friends at a club tomorrow.   a. time
2. What ___ are you going to meet them?   b. come
3. That sounds like fun. Would you mind if I ___ along?   c. kind
4. What ___ of club is it exactly?   d. going
5. It is a ___ club. They have a great DJ.   e. dance

`5`

Unit 8 Test

Name: _____   Date: _____

LISTEN TO THIS

Track 16   **1. A man is talking with his doctor about his new diet. Can he have the following things or not? Listen and check (✓) the correct answer.**

	Can have	Can't have
1. Bacon and sausage		
2. Coffee		
3. Toast and yogurt		
4. Grilled fish		
5. Steaks and burgers		

5

Track 17   **2. People are ordering dinner at a restaurant. Are these statements true or false? Listen and check (✓) the correct answer.**

	True	False
1. The special for the day is a sirloin steak with fries.	☐	☐
2. The special comes with a salad.	☐	☐
3. The restaurant is out of fries.	☐	☐
4. No one orders the special.	☐	☐
5. Everyone is too full to eat dessert.	☐	☐

5

GIVE IT A TRY

1. Write the letter of the correct answer.

1. What's your favorite drink? ___
2. Have you had enough time to look at the menu? ___
3. What do you feel like? ___
4. What do you usually have for breakfast? ___
5. Are you hungry? ___

a. Maybe some Thai food.
b. I guess it's green tea.
c. Not right now.
d. Yes, we're ready to order.
e. I usually have cereal and orange juice.

5

2. Complete each sentence and circle the letter of the correct answer.

1. So what _____ you like to drink?
   a. would
   b. have
   c. is

2. How would you like your steak _____?
   a. eaten
   b. killed
   c. cooked

3. For dessert I'll _____ some chocolate ice cream.
   a. drink
   b. have
   c. am

4. This fish is _____. It is the worst I have ever tasted.
   a. disgusting
   b. delicious
   c. fun

5. That curry is so _____. My tongue is burning!
   a. sweet
   b. sour
   c. spicy

5

Unit 9 Test

Name: _____ Date: _____

LISTEN TO THIS

Track 18 **1.** People are talking. Are these statements true or false? Listen and check (✓) the correct answer.

	True	False
1. The conversation is a job interview.	☐	☐
2. Helen is a very energetic person.	☐	☐
3. Helen is a well-organized person.	☐	☐
4. Helen is probably quite serious.	☐	☐
5. Helen is interested in flexible people.	☐	☐

5

Track 19 **2.** Someone is interviewing for a job at a summer camp. Listen and circle the letter of the correct answer.

1. The applicant is fluent in _____.
   a. Chinese
   b. Spanish
   c. German

2. The applicant is an excellent swimmer and a certified _____.
   a. guardian
   b. lifeguard
   c. singer

3. The applicant can play the _____ and has even written a few songs.
   a. piano
   b. guitar
   c. soccer

4. The applicant is a pretty good _____ as well as a good dancer.
   a. teacher
   b. singer
   c. cook

5. The applicant is one of the _____ people applying for the job.
   a. worst
   b. best
   c. most

5

1. Choose the correct response to each description. Write the letter of
the correct answer.

1. He's patient and he's a good communicator. ___
2. She's creative and has a great sense of style. ___
3. He's good at math and he's well-organized. ___
4. She's really good at drawing and painting. ___
5. He's so funny and entertaining. ___

a. He sounds like a comedian.
b. He must be an accountant.
c. It sounds like she's a great artist.
d. He would be a great teacher.
e. She should be a designer.

5

2. People are talking. Number the sentences in the correct order.

1. ___ B: Sure, that sounds like fun!
2. ___ B: Oh, I don't have plans yet. What about you?
3. ___ A: What are you doing this weekend, Cassy?
4. ___ A: I want to play tennis on Saturday. Do you want to play?
5. ___ A: Great! Let's meet at 1:00.

5

Name: _____ Date: _____

LISTEN TO THIS

Track 20 **1.** Someone is asking where things are. Listen and write the letter of the correct answer.

1. The train station is ___ the corner.
2. The supermarket is next to the ___ on 3rd Avenue.
3. A coffee shop is at ___ Bond Street.
4. The nearest drugstore is on the ___, just past the post office.
5. There is an excellent hotel on the corner of Main and ___.

a. movie theater
b. just around
c. 8th
d. right
e. the end of

5

Track 21 **2.** People are talking about a small town. Are these statements true or false? Listen and check (✓) the correct answer.

	True	False
1. There are five streets in the town.	☐	☐
2. The library is on the corner of Oak and 3rd.	☐	☐
3. The bank is next to the library.	☐	☐
4. The shoe store is on Maple Street.	☐	☐
5. The speaker lives on 3rd Street.	☐	☐

5

GIVE IT A TRY

1. Complete each conversation and circle the letter of the correct answer.

1. A: Can you tell me where the bank is?
   B: The _____ one is on 22nd.

   a. closer
   b. nearest
   c. near

2. A: Where's the movie theater?
   B: It's _____ the corner.

   a. just from
   b. just around
   c. just inside

3. **A:** Excuse me. Where's the bookstore?

   B: It's _____ the parking lot.

   a. across from
   b. left at
   c. behind from

4. **A:** There's a swimming pool downtown, but it's too far to walk.

   B: OK. Should I _____ the subway there?

   a. make
   b. have
   c. take

5. **A:** How do I _____ the music store?

   B: It's three blocks from here.

   a. get to
   b. start from
   c. walk past

5

2. Complete each sentence and circle the letter of the correct answer.

1. Can you _____ me where the zoo is?
   a. believe
   b. find
   c. tell

2. What _____ is Delaware Street?
   a. time
   b. direction
   c. sign

3. Is there a good restaurant _____ this street?
   a. top
   b. inside
   c. on

4. The hospital is _____ the street.
   a. across
   b. into
   c. between

5. Where is the _____ subway station?
   a. funniest
   b. next to
   c. closest

5

Name: _____   Date: _____

LISTEN TO THIS

Track 22   **1. People are asking to borrow things. Are these statements true or false? Listen and check (✓) the correct answer.**

	True	False
1. Julie wants to borrow Shin-uk's car for a date.	☐	☐
2. Tomomi is going to play tennis.	☐	☐
3. Stephanie needs to write a paper.	☐	☐
4. Ken can use Maria's textbook later.	☐	☐
5. Paul can borrow Lisa's DVD player.	☐	☐

5

Track 23   **2. People are asking permission to do things. Choose the correct response to each request. Listen and write the letter of the correct answer.**

1. Mom ____
2. Mr. Wallace ____
3. Lin ____
4. Robert ____
5. Maggie ____

a. Well, I don't like late work, but I guess it's not your fault.
b. As long as there aren't too many people it's OK with me.
c. But I love this show! Can't you wait for ten minutes?
d. I'll have to talk to his mother first.
e. OK, but don't talk too long.

5

1. Write the letter of the correct answer.

1. Why do you need my jacket? ___
2. What do you need the dictionary for? ___
3. Why do you want to borrow my camera? ___
4. Why do you need $20.00? ___
5. Why do you want to borrow my bike? ___

a. I'm broke and I need to eat.
b. I'm going sight-seeing.
c. I'm cold and I forgot mine.
d. I need exercise and mine is broken.
e. I can't understand the meaning of some of these words.

5

2. Complete each sentence and circle the letter of the correct answer.

1. Eric, can I _____ your cell phone? Mine is broken.
   a. lend
   b. borrow
   c. collect

2. Would you _____ if I had some friends come over tonight?
   a. mind
   b. believe
   c. think

3. Is it OK if I _____ the channel? I don't like this TV program.
   a. leave
   b. hold
   c. change

4. I left my wallet at home! Can you _____ me some money?
   a. borrow
   b. lend
   c. contain

5. Can I _____ your bicycle?
   a. use
   b. feel
   c. watch

5

Unit 12 Test

Name: _____   Date: _____

LISTEN TO THIS

Track 24 **1.** Young-mi and Jason are talking about what they did over the summer. Listen and check (✓) the correct answer.

	Young-mi	Jason
1. Took a class		
2. Read some good books		
3. Bought something interesting		
4. Went scuba diving		
5. Traveled to Spain		

5

2. Listen to the conversation again. Circle the letter of the correct answer.

1. Which country was Young-mi's favorite?
   a. Spain
   b. Switzerland
   c. Italy

2. What type of class did Young-mi take?
   a. art history
   b. photography
   c. cooking

3. What was Jason's favorite movie?
   a. *The Secret Lives of Pigeons*
   b. *The Revenge of the Pigeon*
   c. *The Revenge of the Wolfman*

4. What sport did Jason try?
   a. rock climbing
   b. mountain climbing
   c. swimming

5. What did Young-mi buy on vacation?
   a. a jacket
   b. a pair of shoes
   c. books

5

GIVE IT A TRY

1. Complete each sentence with the letter of the correct answer.

1. I really like ___ movies because I like to be scared.
2. What is the ___ thing you have ever done?
3. What kind of movies do you ___?
4. I prefer ___ because I love to laugh.
5. He is not very ___ because he can't tell a joke.

a. scariest
b. like
c. funny
d. horror
e. comedies

5

2. People are talking. Number the sentences in the correct order.

1. ___ **A:** Wow! That's exciting. How long are you going to be there?
2. ___ **A:** What are you going to do this summer, Jo?
3. ___ **B:** I'm going for six weeks. I want to see as much as I can.
4. ___ **A:** Terrific! I hope you have a great time.
5. ___ **B:** I'm going to go to Australia.

5

ANSWER KEY

Unit 1 Test

LISTEN TO THIS 1

1. d   4. b
2. e   5. c
3. a

GIVE IT A TRY 1

1. 5   4. 4
2. 2   5. 3
3. 1

LISTEN TO THIS 2

1. false   4. false
2. true   5. true
3. true

GIVE IT A TRY 2

1. c   4. a
2. e   5. d
3. b

Unit 2 Test

LISTEN TO THIS 1

1. d   4. b
2. e   5. a
3. c

GIVE IT A TRY 1

1. 4   4. 1
2. 2   5. 3
3. 5

LISTEN TO THIS 2

1. e   4. b
2. d   5. c
3. a

GIVE IT A TRY 2

1. c   4. a
2. b   5. c
3. c

Unit 3 Test

LISTEN TO THIS 1

1. e   4. a
2. c   5. d
3. b

GIVE IT A TRY 1

1. c   4. a
2. c   5. b
3. b

LISTEN TO THIS 2

1. false   4. true
2. false   5. false
3. true

GIVE IT A TRY 2

1. b   4. d
2. e   5. c
3. a

Unit 4 Test

LISTEN TO THIS 1

1. d   4. e
2. c   5. b
3. a

GIVE IT A TRY 1

1. b   4. e
2. c   5. d
3. a

LISTEN TO THIS 2

1. c   4. c
2. d   5. d
3. a

GIVE IT A TRY 2

1. a   4. c
2. b   5. b
3. a

Unit 5 Test

LISTEN TO THIS 1

1. c   4. c
2. a   5. d
3. d

GIVE IT A TRY 1

1. c   4. d
2. e   5. b
3. a

LISTEN TO THIS 2

1. false   4. true
2. false   5. true
3. false

GIVE IT A TRY 2

1. b   4. c
2. a   5. b
3. b

Unit 6 Test

LISTEN TO THIS 1

1. false   4. true
2. false   5. false
3. true

GIVE IT A TRY 1

1. b   4. b
2. a   5. c
3. a

LISTEN TO THIS 2

1. a   4. b
2. c   5. d
3. e

GIVE IT A TRY 2

1. e   4. c
2. b   5. a
3. d

Unit 7 Test

LISTEN TO THIS 1

1. true 4. false
2. false 5. true
3. true

LISTEN TO THIS 2

1. e 4. d
2. b 5. a
3. c

GIVE IT A TRY 1

1. c 4. c
2. b 5. a
3. a

GIVE IT A TRY 2

1. d 4. c
2. a 5. e
3. b

Unit 8 Test

LISTEN TO THIS 1

1. can't have 4. can have
2. can't have 5. can't have
3. can have

LISTEN TO THIS 2

1. false 4. true
2. true 5. false
3. true

GIVE IT A TRY 1

1. b 4. e
2. d 5. c
3. a

GIVE IT A TRY 2

1. a 4. a
2. c 5. c
3. b

Unit 9 Test

LISTEN TO THIS 1

1. false 4. false
2. true 5. true
3. false

LISTEN TO THIS 2

1. a 4. c
2. b 5. b
3. a

GIVE IT A TRY 1

1. d 4. c
2. e 5. a
3. b

GIVE IT A TRY 2

1. 4 4. 3
2. 2 5. 5
3. 1

Unit 10 Test

LISTEN TO THIS 1

1. b 4. d
2. a 5. c
3. e

LISTEN TO THIS 2

1. true 4. false
2. false 5. true
3. true

GIVE IT A TRY 1

1. b 4. c
2. b 5. a
3. a

GIVE IT A TRY 2

1. c 4. a
2. b 5. c
3. c

Unit 11 Test

LISTEN TO THIS 1

1. false 4. true
2. false 5. false
3. true

LISTEN TO THIS 2

1. d 4. e
2. a 5. c
3. b

GIVE IT A TRY 1

1. c 4. b
2. e 5. d
3. b

GIVE IT A TRY 2

1. b 4. b
2. a 5. a
3. c

Unit 12 Test

LISTEN TO THIS 1

1. Young-mi 4. Jason
2. Jason 5. Young-mi
3. Young-mi

LISTEN TO THIS 2

1. b 4. a
2. a 5. a
3. c

GIVE IT A TRY 1

1. d 4. e
2. a 5. c
3. b

GIVE IT A TRY 2

1. 3 4. 5
2. 1 5. 2
3. 4

Unit 1 Test

LISTEN TO THIS

Track 2

1

1.

H: Hi. My name is Hidetoshi Soda. What's your name?

W: My name is Mr. Moon. But you can call me Won-gyu.

2.

F: I'm your teacher this week. My name is Fred Manson. But you can call me Fred.

T: Hi, Fred. I'm Ted.

F: What's your last name?

T: My last name is Robinson.

3.

L: Good morning.

M: Good morning.

L: What's your name again?

M: My name is Miho Honda. And your name is Lisa Wu, right?

L: Yeah. That's right.

4.

E: See you later, Yuko.

Y: Good-bye, Mrs. Miller.

E: Yuko, please call me Emily.

5.

D: Hello, Barry.

B: Hi. How are you, Mr. Kozo?

D: Please don't call me Mr. Kozo. Just call me Dan.

Track 3

2

N: Sue, who's that girl?

S: Oh, that's Mari.

N: Who's she?

S: She's Noriko's sister.

N: She's really pretty.

S: Do you want to meet her?

N: You bet I do.

S: Hey, Mari. This is my friend Nat.

M: Hi, Nat. Nice to meet you.

N: Nice to meet you, too.

M: Are you in my math class?

N: Yes, I am.

Unit 2 Test

LISTEN TO THIS

Track 4

1

1.

A: Those are cool sneakers. What sports do you use them for?

B: Well, they're good for basketball, but I don't really play.

2.

A: Are these your keys? I found them on the sidewalk.

B: Yes, they are. Thank you very much. I need them to get into my house.

3.

A: That's a big backpack. Is it heavy?

B: Yes, I have all my textbooks in it.

4.

A: I like your jacket. Is it very warm?

B: Yes, it is. I wear it when I go skiing.

5.

A: Those are great earrings. Where did you get them?

B: My mother gave them to me.

Track 5

2

A: Have you seen my green shirt?

B: It's in the closet.

A: How about my cell phone?

B: You left it on the kitchen table.

A: Have you seen my bag?

B: It's next to the couch where you left it last night.

A: Thanks. Um, do you know where my keys are?

B: They're in the pocket of your jacket.

A: One more thing. Have you seen my sunglasses?

B: They're on top of your head!

A: Thanks. I have to go to work now. I'll see you tonight.

B: Wait! Don't forget your shoes.

A: Oh, right. See you later.

Unit 3 Test

LISTEN TO THIS

Track 6

1

1.

A: OK, let me ask you a few questions. What's your name?

B: Brian Davidson.

A: And what sports are you interested in training for?

B: Well, I run track and I'm trying to increase my speed.

A: OK, before we get started, I just need to know how old you are.

B: I'm 21.

2.

A: And what is your name?

C: Hyun-young Choi.

A: And how old are you?

C: I just turned 20 last week.

A: And what sports are you interested in training for?

C: I don't like sports. I just want to get into better shape.

3.

D: Hi, my name is Anna Nelson.

A: How can I help you, Anna?

D: Well, I'd like to play basketball.

A: How tall are you?

D: I'm 180 centimeters.

A: And your age?

D: I'm 24 years old.

4.

E: Hi, I'd like to play baseball.

A: And what is your name?

E: Shoji Fujimori.

A: How much do you weigh, Shoji?

E: I'm about 58 kilos.

A: And how old are you?

E: I'm 23.

5.

F: Hi, my name is Pavel Hoffman. I'm 22 years old. I weigh 60 kilos, and I'm 170 centimeters tall.

A: OK, Pavel, and what sports are interested in playing?

F: I like all sports, but I think I want to play hockey the most.

Track 7

2

L: So, why don't you tell me about yourself, Andy?

A: Well, I come from a small family. I have only one older brother.

L: How old is your brother?

A: Well, I'm 23 and he is three years older, so I guess he's 26 now.

L: What do you like to do in your free time?

A: Well, I love baseball, and I really enjoy reggae music.

L: Me, too. Well, not baseball, but I love reggae and hip-hop.

A: How about you, Li-wei? Do you come from a big family?

L: Yes, I have four younger sisters and one older brother.

A: That is a big family!

Unit 4 Test

LISTEN TO THIS

Track 8

1

1.

A: Who is that girl over there?

B: Which one?

A: The one with curly black hair, in the green sweater.

B: Oh, that's Mary.

2.

A: Which one is your boss?

B: The blonde guy near the pool in the yellow T-shirt.

A: What's his name?

B: Mr. Davidson.

3.

A: Can I see your photos?

B: Sure.

A: Wow! Who is this girl in the red dress with the long brown hair?

B: Oh, that's my cousin Jessie.

4.

A: I know that guy from somewhere.

B: Which one?

A: The short heavy guy with glasses.

B: Oh yeah, he works with Jim. His name is David Kline.

5.

A: Has anyone seen my wife, So-hyun?

B: What does she look like?

A: She's short and thin with long black hair, and she's wearing a pink skirt.

B: Oh, I think I saw her over by the pool talking with your boss.

Track 9

2

A: Mike, did you get gifts for everyone in the family?

B: Yeah, I just need to wrap them now.

A: What did you get Dad?

B: I got him a blue-and-red-striped tie.

A: That sounds nice. What did you get for Jenny?

B: I got her a cute little red coat. It's very warm.

A: Oh, that sounds perfect. Did you get anything for Jeremy?

B: Yeah, I got him a pair of dark brown dress shoes to match his new suit.

A: Good idea, he really needs those. How about Allison?

B: Oh, I got her that new pair of blue jeans she's been asking for.

A: And what about Grandma?

B: I got her a silver bracelet with her name on it.

Unit 5 Test

LISTEN TO THIS

Track 10

1

1.

A: I'm so tired. I didn't get to bed until 2:00 A.M. last night. I really need to get more sleep.

B: I know what you mean. If I don't get at least eight hours every night, I can't function the next day.

2.

A: Hey, do you know what time this class is going to end?

B: It's supposed to end at a quarter after three.

3.

A: What time does that movie begin tonight?

B: According to the newspaper, it starts at half past eight on channel 12.

4.

A: What time do you have to get up in the morning?

B: During the week I have to get out of bed by 6:30.

5.

A: What time did you make our dinner reservations for?

B: We're supposed to be at the restaurant at a quarter to seven.

Track 11

2

1.

A: Jung-soon, what do you usually do on the weekend?

B: Well, I work every Saturday, but I usually try and go to the park to relax on Sunday.

2.

A: Hey Minako, I haven't seen you in a while. Why don't we go out for lunch after class today?

B: Oh, Toshi. I'd like to go, but I have tickets for the baseball game right after school. Maybe we can go out to lunch next week.

3.

A: Eva, I haven't seen you in such a long time. Where have you been?

B: Oh, I took a vacation from school and went to Italy for my sister's wedding.

4.

A: Jade, I'm having a party at my house on Saturday. Can you come?

B: I'd love to. Should I bring anything to the party?

A: No, we have everything we need. Just bring yourself.

5.

A: Hyun-gil, what are you going to do tonight?

B: Well, I have a big test tomorrow, so I'll probably have to study all night.

Unit 6 Test

LISTEN TO THIS

Track 12

1

J: So, Young-su, what do you do?

Y: Well, I'm studying French at night and going to cooking school during the day. How about you, Julia?

J: I just started at City College last year.

Y: What's your major?

J: I'm still undecided. I'm taking several classes and trying to figure out what I like best. So far, engineering is my favorite class.

Y: That sounds interesting.

J: Yeah, it is. So, how do you like cooking school?

Y: It's OK, but I have a lot to learn.

J: Well, maybe you can practice by cooking for me some time!

Track 13

2

A: Who is your favorite professor?

B: Well, I really like Professor Chen. His lessons are interesting, and he's so funny.

A: That's true. He is funny, but his lessons don't really prepare me for his tests.

B: Well, I also like Professor Marx. She has a really unique teaching style and is always available to answer questions after class.

A: Yes, but she's so serious. I don't think I've ever seen her smile.

B: Well, how about Professor Riddle? He's always in a good mood.

A: Yeah, but he usually comes to class late, and he's never there during his office hours. He's really unreliable.

B: OK, well I also like Professor Johnson. He's very easygoing and reliable.

A: Oh, I can't stand his classes, he is so boring.

B: Well, who do you like?

A: I think Professor Houston is the best teacher at this school. His classes are fascinating.

B: You're just saying that because he's your father.

Unit 7 Test

LISTEN TO THIS

Track 14

1

S: So, Yoshi, what do you usually do on the weekend?

Y: Well, New York is such an exciting city. I often see live music on Friday night. How about you, Sarah?

S: I love seeing shows on Broadway. Have you been to many?

Y: Not really. I saw one when I first moved here and then another when my parents came to visit, but none since then. What do you usually do on Saturday and Sunday?

S: On Saturday I like to go to the park and relax. I usually see a movie on Saturday night. What do you do?

Y: I play tennis on Saturday. Unfortunately, I have to work every Sunday.

S: How about the opera? Have you ever been to one at Lincoln Center?

Y: You know, I've never seen an opera in my life.

S: Oh, you should! Why don't we go see *Don Giovanni* next week?

Y: That sounds like fun to me.

Track 15

2

A: Hey Tamara, how did you spend your weekend?

B: Well, on Friday we went to the City Museum and saw some interesting exhibitions. And then on Saturday, I went shopping and bought a great new pair of shoes. How about you, Arun? What did you do last weekend?

A: Well, I saw a baseball game on Friday. That was really exciting. And then on Saturday night, I met some friends and we went out to dinner downtown.

B: Did you do anything on Sunday?

A: I basically studied all day Sunday because I have a big test coming up on Wednesday. How about you, did you do anything on Sunday?

B: Not really. I was so tired that I slept until 2:00 in the afternoon.

Unit 8 Test

LISTEN TO THIS

Track 16

1

A: I'm afraid we are going to have to put you on a strict diet. From now on, you cannot drink any coffee, and you are going to have to stay away from salty foods.

B: Does that mean I can't have any more fast food?

A: Absolutely not. You can't have any fried foods and you need to stay away from hamburgers and steaks as well.

B: What about breakfast foods like bacon, eggs, and sausage?

A: I'm sorry, but those are all bad for you. You can have cereal, toast, yogurt, and orange juice for breakfast.

B: Well, what about lunch and dinner?

A: Have a salad for lunch. You can eat all the vegetables you want as well. Grilled fish and chicken are also OK.

B: What about dessert? Can I still have ice cream?

A: Yes, but not too much, and frozen yogurt would be better.

Track 17

2

A: Good evening. First, I'd like to tell you about today's special. It's a grilled tuna steak with a mixed green salad on the side. And for dessert we have a fresh fruit plate.

B: Thanks, I think I'd actually like a club sandwich with a side of fries and a soda.

A: I'm sorry, we're all out of fries. Would you like a baked potato instead?

B: That's fine, I guess.

C: I'd like the seafood salad to start, a toasted cheese sandwich, and an iced tea.

A: And for you, sir?

D: I'll have the chicken wings and a side of macaroni and cheese.

A: Would you like anything for dessert?

D: Nothing for me, thanks. I'm sure I'll be too full for dessert.

C: Not me. I'll have a slice of the strawberry cheesecake. It looks delicious.

B: And I'd like a slice of apple pie with cinnamon ice cream.

Unit 9 Test

LISTEN TO THIS

Track 18

1

A: So, Helen, how would you describe yourself?

B: Well, I think that I'm pretty easygoing, and generous with my time when it comes to my friends and family. I'm also a very energetic person and I have a lot of enthusiasm for many things. At least, that's what my friends say.

A: What would you say are your worst qualities?

B: Well, I do tend to try and do too much at once, so sometimes I'm not reliable. And I'm definitely not well-organized.

A: And what are the qualities that you're looking for in a roommate?

B: Well, I guess I want to live with someone who is also energetic, and I really like creative people. I think it's also important that a person can be flexible and understanding when I make mistakes.

A: Are there any qualities that you cannot tolerate in another person?

B: I really hate it when people are too serious and have no sense of humor.

Track 19

2

A: OK, for this position we need really well-rounded people with a variety of talents.

B: Well, to begin with, I can play the piano very well and have even written several songs.

A: That's good to hear. Do you speak any other languages?

B: Well, my parents are from Taiwan, so I'm fluent in Chinese. And I've just started studying Spanish as well.

A: OK, and how about sports, are you very athletic?

B: Well, I played soccer for five years, and I'm an excellent swimmer and a certified lifeguard.

A: Great, we need a lifeguard. Do you have any other special talents that you think might be useful to us?

B: I'm a pretty good cook, and I'm a very good salsa dancer as well.

A: Well, I just have to speak with a few more people, but you are definitely one of our best applicants.

Unit 10 Test

LISTEN TO THIS

Track 20

1

A: Excuse me. I'm visiting for a few days and I don't know how to get around. Can you tell me where the train station is?

B: Sure, it's just around the corner on Market Street.

A: Can you also tell me how to get to the supermarket?

B: There's one next to the movie theater on 3rd Avenue.

A: Do you know if there's a good coffee shop around here?

B: Sure, there's one at the end of Bond Street on the right. It's called Java City.

A: How about the nearest drugstore?

B: There is one on the right, just past the post office.

A: One more thing. I'm looking for a good hotel. Do you know of any in the area?

B: Yes, there's an excellent hotel on the corner of Main and 8th.

A: Thanks so much for your help.

B: No problem. Enjoy your stay.

Track 21

2

A: OK. There are two main streets in our town. Their names are Oak and Maple, and they are connected by the three streets 1st, 2nd, and 3rd.

B: And where is the library?

A: The library is on the corner of Oak and 1st Street.

B: And where is the bank?

A: Oh, it's right next to the library on 1st.

B: Where is a shoe store?

A: Well, we don't have a shoe store in town. You have to go to the next town.

B: Do you have a post office?

A: Yes, we do. It's in the center of town in the middle of 2nd Street.

B: And where do you live?

A: I live on 3rd Street close to Maple.

Unit 11 Test

LISTEN TO THIS

Track 22

1

1.

A: Hey, Shin-uk, can I ask you for a favor?

B: Sure, Julie. What is it?

A: Well, my dad is flying into town tomorrow and I need to pick him up at the airport. Can I borrow your car?

B: Oh, I have a date tomorrow, so I need my car. Sorry!

2.

A: Tomomi, are you going to play tennis tonight?

B: I don't think so. Why?

A: Well, I wanted to play tennis tonight, but I can't find my racket. Can I borrow yours?

B: Sure. No problem.

3.

A: John, would you mind if I borrowed your laptop?

B: When do you need it, Stephanie?

A: I have a paper due tomorrow and I need to work on it all night.

B: Actually, I'll be using it tonight. I have to write a paper, too.

4.

A: Hi, Maria. Can I borrow your textbook? I didn't bring mine today.

B: Well, Ken, I'm using it now. Can I lend it to you later?

A: Yeah. Thanks a lot.

5.

A: Hey, Lisa. Can I borrow your DVD player?

B: Oh, sorry, Paul. It's not working.

A: That's too bad. Thanks anyway.

Track 23

2

1.

A: Hey, Mom. Would it be OK if I stayed over at Kevin's house tonight? His parents are going to be there and I'll call you before I go to bed.

2.

B: Excuse me, Mr. Wallace. I have a problem. I know my paper is due on Friday, but my computer broke last night and I lost all my work. Could I turn the paper in on Monday?

3.

C: Hey, Lin. I was thinking about having some friends come over to our place on Saturday night for a party, but I wanted to see if it was OK with you first.

4.

D: Robert, can I borrow your phone for a minute? I forgot mine at home again and I need to make a quick call to Dennis.

5.

E: You know what, Maggie? If you don't change the channel, I'll tell Mom and Dad that you haven't studied for your test tomorrow.

Unit 12 Test

LISTEN TO THIS

Track 24

Y: Hey, Jason. It's good to see you. How was your summer? Did you do anything special?

J: Well, it was really relaxing. I spent a lot of time at the beach. How about you, Young-mi? What did you do with your summer?

Y: Oh, I had a really exciting summer. I took a class at City College and I traveled to Europe.

J: What class did you take?

Y: I took an art history class. It was really interesting.

J: And where did you travel in Europe?

Y: I went to Germany, France, Spain, Italy, and Switzerland.

J: Wow, which was your favorite?

Y: Well, I think I liked the mountains of Switzerland the best. It was the most beautiful for me. France had the best food, in my opinion, but I enjoyed something about each place. So, did you just hang out at the beach all summer?

J: Well, I also read a lot of good books, and saw some movies as well. Oh, and I tried rock climbing a few times and even went scuba diving once.

Y: That sounds like fun. What books did you read?

J: Well my favorite was *The Secret Lives of Pigeons*. I thought it was very funny.

Y: Oh, I've never heard of that. What was the best movie of the summer?

J: I'd have to say that *The Revenge of the Wolfman* was my favorite. It was such a beautiful love story, so romantic, I cried at the end. So, did you buy anything interesting in Europe?

Y: Yes, I bought a very nice leather jacket in Italy. I can't wait for the weather to get cool so I can wear it. Well, I have to go to class now. I'll see you later.

TRACK LIST

TRACK	CONTENT
1	Title and copyright
2	Unit 1, Listen to This 1
3	Unit 1, Listen to This 2
4	Unit 2, Listen to This 1
5	Unit 2, Listen to This 2
6	Unit 3, Listen to This 1
7	Unit 3, Listen to This 2
8	Unit 4, Listen to This 1
9	Unit 4, Listen to This 2
10	Unit 5, Listen to This 1
11	Unit 5, Listen to This 2
12	Unit 6, Listen to This 1

TRACK	CONTENT
13	Unit 6, Listen to This 2
14	Unit 7, Listen to This 1
15	Unit 7, Listen to This 2
16	Unit 8, Listen to This 1
17	Unit 8, Listen to This 2
18	Unit 9, Listen to This 1
19	Unit 9, Listen to This 2
20	Unit 10, Listen to This 1
21	Unit 10, Listen to This 2
22	Unit 11, Listen to This 1
23	Unit 11, Listen to This 2
24	Unit 12, Listen to This 1 and 2